honey *learning to live in liquid love*

honey

learning to live in liquid love

a book of poems by **ALLY LONG**

TABLE OF CONTENTS

DEDICATION

For those who opened this book wondering if
maybe I wrote it for them... for the ones needing to
feel seen by the words on these pages and the One
they are written about:

Read on
Slowly or all at once
Let your eyes eat
Your soul be watered
Your heart be comforted
Your spirit be encouraged

And, dear reader, I promise you with everything
in me, it is worth it. Receive Jesus in each painful
place and those places will change (and you with
them). If you don't know Him, ask Him to make
Himself real to you.

Welcome to healing.

"Gracious words are a honeycomb,
sweet to the soul and healing to the bones."

Proverbs 16:24 NIV

prologue: **GARDEN CONVERSATIONS**

how is she doing today
they asked—bumble bees—drifting to the flowers
near my toes

she's learning to rest
said the Father, smoothing stray hairs
from my sleeping face

we saw her, said the lilies,
running through the fields yesterday
to the house in her heart

yes, He said, pleased,
we meet there often

we found her lying in the meadow by the stream—
a bee bumbled to the Man
sleeping—another added

but her cheeks were salty—they whispered
there was a great rain on our flowers where her head rested

carrying her back to the house, He said,
she is learning to grieve well

if you make the honey, He said to the bees,
I'll use it to anoint her lips
it will mark her words
and drip from her hands

this is how we flourish
the wildflowers said, demonstrating—

we drink His water
we eat His light
we push push push our roots
down into His heart
(it's what grounds us, makes us strong)
we let His life-words rest on our petals
orange-blue-white

they watched her in approval and beamed—
yes, that's right

the great pines stirred with pride
leaning near their neighbors—did you see her
catch those troubling foxes?

didn't you see—
that Man that glows was helping her,
the other trees whispered in awe—
they did it together

the deer watched and whispered (wide eyed)
from the edge of the clearing
as the Spirit led her up the porch steps,

the Man opened the door and hugged her, helping her inside and
pointing up the stairs (where the Father was waiting for her)
He looked at the spot from where they watched and winked

together they watched her
is she building a nest?
the sparrows asked the Spirit

close, He said as the Father helped her—
she is building an altar

the sunflowers turned to watch
as she and the Father
walked together among them one morning

He sparkles, said one sunflower
so does she, said another

"Eat honey, my son, for it is good;
honey from the comb is sweet to your taste.
Know also that wisdom is like honey for you:
if you find it, there is a future hope for you,
and your hope will not be cut off."

Proverbs 24:13-14 NIV

part 1: **ME**

THE HOUSE IN MY HEART

A friend once taught me
About a secret place
The house in my heart
It stands tall and warm and white
It has a great front porch
And the door is Jesus
And beyond Him is glowing light

My house has
A sunroom upstairs where I meet the Father
(I tell Him my secrets He already knew
And He tells me some secrets too)
A bathroom where we wash
(The blood works)
A kitchen where we feast
A bedroom where we sleep
And a balcony in the back that overlooks a forest

Beyond that forest is a stream
Beyond that stream is a meadow
And we watch it all as we sit on our porch swing
And all the windows are wide open
Because the wind is the Spirit
And He blows continually

HONEY

Her words were so beautiful
They would kiss her just to taste them

Her words were so beautiful that
Each beholder's eyes filled with tears and those tears
Spilled over warm, glowing cheeks, planting seeds

Her words were so beautiful
They flowed like honey
Over the lips of the ones who loved her
Into the crevices of their hearts

Her words were so beautiful because
The One who inspired them is beauty Himself
You become what you behold
You eat with your eyes
You are what you eat...

Out of the heart, the mouth speaks

Out of a beautiful heart
Words will taste like honey

If there's anything I've learned, dear reader,
It is that if my heart came alive,
And I learned to wordsmith with Jesus
And beauty comes from ashes,
You can too.

ON HEALING I

It's not perfect
It's not pretty
It's not simple
But it is beautiful
   It is lovely
   It is refining
   It is humbling
   It is a lot of forgiveness
   It is a lot of releasing
   A lot of letting go
      Letting yourself know
      You're forgiven
   It is a lot of being honest
   And if we're being honest,
Healing is hard
Healing is not convenient
Healing takes heart work; hard work
Healing takes trust
Trust that it is worth it
     Trust that letting go
       Makes you more full
Healing takes more time than you would think
   It is giving it all to the One
   And letting Him hold you when you weep

And letting Him wipe away your tears
And letting Him take your fears
Putting a crown on your head
       A golden crown of righteousness and royalty
           A crown you think doesn't belong
           But He thinks should have been there
           all along

Healing
It takes finding yourself worthy of mercy
It takes finding yourself worthy of grace
It takes forgetting how to put on a brave face
      And letting Him hold you
Letting Him come close
Letting Him be near
Letting Him whisper in your ear
Telling you how proud He is of you
Loves you
Delights in you
Is refreshed by you.
      "Abba, can you come hold me now?"
      I'm here, baby girl.

CAPTIVATED

My Beloved's gaze is fire,
Of looking in His eyes
I never tire

MAY I'S

Oh Lord, may I be more caught up in what You think of me
Than what others are currently thinking

May I be so intoxicated with Your presence on a daily basis
That others get intoxicated too
May my life be permission for others to experience You

Oh Lord, may I be so enthralled by Your beauty
That other beautiful things dim in comparison

May I be so immersed in Your heart
That coming out of it would feel like drowning
But Lord, may I never leave the oxygen of Your love.

NUMB

The sky cries the tears I want to

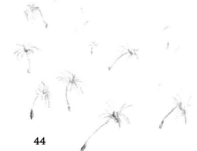

POLLINATING KINDNESS

What if kindness was like pollen?
Would love and consideration drip off our tongues
like carefully cultivated honey
Or roll down our fingertips in excess like raindrops,
Falling in that hurried way from flower petals after a fresh rain?
Watering the ground and nourishing the heart...
We all need to play our part
Would our love spread like spring's pollen in open air?
Look at how we love.
Would it look like flowers blooming in a bright room?
Would our kindness be to those around us a sweet-smelling perfume?

A GIFT

Those who cry with you

TRAPPED

My heart races—I spin on and on for hours
The heaviness pressing on my chest and the
Swirling vortex of thoughts in my mind
Keep me in my introspection and overthinking
Unable to escape

In my weakness
You poke the heart-space
In my chest I thought
You had abandoned, and
My spirit leaps in response with a flicker of hope

You blow gently
Into my heart

The swirling slows
And I finally can breathe freely
Oh, what a relief it is
The Prince of Peace never left me

INVITATION

Oh, what an ocean
Grace abounds in rising swells
A gentle, whisper-like, almost playful tug on your legs as you walk—
Almost too playful for the deep ache of need inside you—
Deeper still out to the horizon
Oh, the vastness of His mercy
Heart and body, spirit and soul preserved
In this collection of salt water you've offered Him
Unexplored life teeming in the depths
Grace abounds here in the swells...
Lose yourself in them.

HOUSE OF REVELATION

There is a place
A secret space
Where He shows His face

GRATITUDE

Beyond the circumstances—practice this

FAMILIARITY

I look at You and
My restless spirit settles once again.
Why did I ever look away?

Keep my gaze fixed on You always.
Thank you for choice, Lord,
But I have found what I want.

Tie me to Your hand.
If You don't go with me,
I won't go.

Hold my face steady
And let my eyes always
Be fixed only on You.

Find me at rest
With my eyes opened wide—
How could I ever look away?

ON HEALING II

It's still a process,
It's still intensive and deep
There are hard days and bad days,
                    Sad days and painful days
                    Days when loneliness tries to lie
                    To your heart
                    About who you are
                          And what you can do
                          And who really loves you.
There are still days you doubt
And wonder if the One who led you in here
                          Will ever bring you out.
But healing is also a process
            Still-Healing means you have made progress
You may not be finished
You may not feel different
But there is One who finishes what He starts
Every time
I know this because He made me a promise
        I have spoken, and I will do it
        So I trust Him.
Still-Healing also means that there are good days with the bad days
                          And glimpses into the light

And sometimes when I
feel hopeless
I wait for Hope to come to me
And He does, every single time.
He catches every tear
Until all my blurry eyes can see
Is the shoulder of the One who holds me
And all I can feel is the warmth of His chest
The compassion of His
heart
The radiance of His glory
The comfort of His Spirit
And the closeness of His arms
around me
My King,
Holding me.

RECIPROCATE

Be gentle with yourself
For He is gentle with you

LIES

They're like ugly outdated wallpaper
Let Him tear them down

DOUBT

We don't always get the point
But trust in the One who is Good
He completes every sentence with love

LEAN

Into Grace and
Listen to His heart
Grace is a Man
His work in us is a
Work of art

LESSONS

Sorrow is a good teacher
She teaches that life goes on
        Through tragedy and grief
She shows her true colors in the night
And how joy comes in the mourning

Suffering is harder to learn from
She shows what it's like to sit in real pain
        To endure for heaven's claim
Because you must see past her
        To the One who gave you these companions
She teaches how to wrestle with questions
        And about overcoming doubt to find peace

But most of all,
Sorrow and Suffering teach a song
One that can only rise from within the deep
They teach,
        "One breath, one day at a time"
        "You breathe in YHWH to breathe out love"
        "Even here, Little One, is an offering to give"

They teach of adoration strong enough to overcome torment
And then they prove His great adoration for you

INCLINATION

Even the rainbows
Wild light-water
Submit to His Lordship
Their posture is reverence

DECLUTTERING

Even when you feel fear
You don't have to give into it
Even when you can't hear Him
            He speaks to you
Sometimes it's just a matter of
Clearing out the clutter
Taking every thought captive
            And knowing what He sounds like
            To hear, to get rid of the fear
Because Perfect Love, He sounds kind
He gently corrects
And lovingly points out what Truth is
            He allows light to pour in
            And draws you in with His grace
            Instead of pushing you away with shame
And that's the difference
Between the Perfect Love
And the fear that's been speaking in your ear
            One sounds like peace
            The other sounds like defeat
            And you have the power to choose
            What you listen to

ON HEALING III

So it's been almost a year
Since I let the healing begin
It wasn't perfect
And I felt weak most of the time
But also most of the time
I had support
I had help
I wasn't alone
       Though I felt alone at times
I don't think healing has an end, but
In the end, I've realized
Healing should happen for everyone
Everyone should have the moments to exchange
       The brokenness for the whole
       The trauma for the peace
       The hurt for the healing
       Old memories for new ones
       Fear for trust
       Anger for gentleness
       Bitterness for forgiveness
Healing is always happening, if you let Him

Some seasons are more intense than others
And it's hard
It's humbling
But to feel again—that is worth it
Healing is really just beauty from the inside out
Coming alive again

CREAM AND SUGAR

Today I met Him in the kitchen,
Inside my sanctified imagination.
He made me coffee, and then sat next to me at the counter.
I leaned back on His chest—sinking into the
Rise, fall, rise, fall
of His life-giving breath—
I have never known a man so warm.
We talked about the condition of my heart
I could feel His chest rumbling with the vibration of His voice—
Thunder and lightning—
Safety here in this morning moment

AFFIRMATION TO LIVE

Someone needs to see that they are not alone
Someone needs to see their past is not
Their future written in stone
Someone needs to know who they are in Truth

Someone needs to feel forgiveness running deeply through
Someone needs to try to live and breathe another day
And see Hope coming to them,
Pointing out the way

Someone needs to cry and grieve and know that it's okay
Someone needs to look at the One who takes
This pain away
And just gaze on His beauty

Because strangely enough
When we tell Him our story
In His radiance and glory
Everything else grows dim

REMEMBRANCE

There is permission
In the bread—broken—
And in the wine—spilled—
To be whole

It means
I belong
To Him and
I am whole
In Him

It means
I am healed
Because of Him and
I am covered
Because His life
Is now mine too

ON HEALING IV

Healing is day by day
Breath by breath
Inhale, breathe in, and the broken glass expands
Exhale, breath out, and His presence presses it in close
His very essence holding the shattered heart together
Shards of sharp glass
Inhale and expand
      He comes in the midst of the pain
Exhale and contract
      The shards hurt and the ache is there
      But the King is too
      The Prince of Peace
      The Perfect God-Man Jesus
      In the midst
Day to day
As surely as the sun will rise
He is faithful
He walks among the lampstands
He is in the middle
He doesn't pass you by
He notices when you grab the hem of His robe
      And stops to call you by name
Healing is a journey
Healing is meeting this Man all over again

Healing is a winding road of ups and downs
And in the pain and the heartache
The One who holds your heart together
Gives you promises along the way
Small kisses that tether you to His heart

RESCUED

From behind
He walks inside my
Memories—on an instant replay loop
Called trauma

He puts His left hand on my forehead
And encircles my chest with
His right hand, holding my heart
And He lifts me up out of the memory

In this hug from behind
His right cheek smushes against my left temple
His salt-water-grief-compassion
Mixes with mine

And I remember again
Because I had forgotten—trauma does this—
While I was reliving my past instead of living my present
That the Man Jesus is real

FALSE ENTITLEMENT

Holding on too tight looks like
Mourning over time I thought I had, but never got
      When I never really had that right
Stinging from the crescent-shaped fingernail marks
I've made in the palms of my hands
      Gripping with weak might

But when I said I would follow my Beloved,
It means coming under His covering:
Vulnerability—humility—displayed in His open, nail-pierced hands,
      It means I committed to releasing what I held too tight

So this is where I am now
Imperfectly mirroring my Maker
      Learning humility and walking in the light

SABBATH

Warm: Water
Waves: Washing
Sand: Skin
Salt: Wind
Peace: Still

THE FREE ARTIST

There are some days when lies will seem
Louder than they should
And the ache starts to ache deeper
Than you thought it would
But this just proves
How brightly you'll shine
When you finally start coloring
Outside of the lines

HEARTBREAK

Storms rise from within
Torrents of hope toss to and fro
Thoughts become tornadoes inside
Waves of grief swell from behind

Crashing over your head in
Cold reality
Drowning your eyes in salt-water tears which
Cleanse the ache and the hurt and the pain—somehow—

And from the inside His goodness comes down
Pouring out
In a great thick sheet of heart-aching
Fresh-water-love-rain

THE MIDNIGHT HOURS

I remember so clearly meeting God there
Desperate — laying on the carpeted floor of my room at 1am
Silently weeping (my abandoned effort of holding the tidal
wave inside)

Tears streaming uncontrolled
Rolling into my hair, warm and wet
As loneliness stole my joy from me

I remember asking God
Why broken hearts hurt so much
Accusing Him of letting me fall in love

And warmth came, pressing through my hurt and confusion
as He said,

> *Baby girl, you're allowed to wrestle with Me,*
> *But just let Me hug you right now*

THE FULLNESS

Sanctified
Even our imaginations

ON COMPASSION I

Seeing their spirit
Instead of
Seeing their flesh

VOWS

And if my heart tosses
Back and forth
Like waves of ocean,
It is there I vow
To draw near
To open up my heart
To let the gaze of my Bridegroom
Settle
Any waves into
Perfect Peace (the Man)
I, His, and He, mine.
It is here I rest

UNDERSTANDING

Even now, in the middle of the chaos,
I am learning to root and grow
I am learning to understand the words,
            Be still and know

RESURRECTED

Graveyards sing no songs, but I do

PASSIONATE

There is a Man
He is trustworthy and true
And His eyes of fire are
Fixed on you

ROOTING

Is the extending down
The reaching
The grasping
Into the ground
From where you came
Deeper into the idea "foundation"
Rooting is the hungry searching
The remembering and
The clinging to
Who you are and
Who made you

SEASONS

Summer: Moon
River: Rest
Fall: Blanket
Sleep: Dream
Winter: Snow
Walk: Light
Spring: Alive
Laugh: Bright

TRANSITION

Slow and fast
All at once—hurry up and wait
An intense
Catching up to reality
Like the stage of childbirth called transition
Things are happening
I can't control them
My body responds before
My head and my heart
Trembling, shaking—
As God facilitates the
Outward and downward movement
Of the beauty I've been growing within—
But I know
I will birth something beautiful

MAGIC

When we stop trying to be like other people

PICNIC

Today in my sanctified imagination He was waiting for me
In the fields of blue-orange-white wildflowers
Pollen swirling into the strands of my hair as I approached Him

I laid down next to Him
As He kept His eyes closed but smiled in greeting
I let out a sigh
And He did too
I rolled over on my side to look at Him, Jesus,
And I could see the rise fall, rise fall of His chest
        And the almost imperceptible bounce of His very
        real heart beating

His very real eyes opened to look at me, beaming
Brown-blue light

ON COMPASSION II

The tears of the Father reigning on my head
As I ask him if I should be feeling these emotions like this and
He responds right then
    It's okay, Little One, to be the way I made you

TENSION

Even though there is a risk of
Pain
Heartbreak
Loss
Rejection

The greatest gift you can give someone
Is to let
       them
              know
                     you.

ABANDONED HOUSE

Just take a deep breath
In the here and now
As long as you are breathing,
You still have life to live
As long as you keep living
Love will keep finding you
And coming through the cracks of
The windows you boarded up
        The walls you built
        The shame and guilt
It's relieving to be found right where you are
For someone to see through
        The boarded-up windows
        The ugly lie-walls
Remove the boards
Open up the door
He's waiting on the porch

ETERNAL LIFE

Upon sin forever
It is His
Victorious-wrap-around love-covering

His great vengeance
Upon every shadow
And even Death itself

"So I've learned from my experience
that God protects the vulnerable.
For I was broken and brought low,
but he answered me and came to my rescue!
Now I can say to myself and to all
'Relax and rest, be confident and serene,
For the Lord rewards fully those who
simply trust in him.' God has rescued
my soul from death's fear
and dried my eyes of many tears.
He's kept my feet firmly on his path
And strengthened me so that I may
please him and walk before Yahweh
in his fields of life."

Psalms 116: 6-9 TPT

Selah

INTERLUDE I

He's like walking outside
On one of the first spring days when
The radiant warm sun beams — at last —
Flood your face

INTERLUDE II

He's like a hot shower
After the hardest day
Peace washing over you in torrents of
Hot-liquid love-rain

INTERLUDE III

He's like that reunion hug with your dad
Squeezed too tight
Burying your face in his chest
Breathing in safety at last

INTERLUDE IV

He's like a freshly changed bed
And the sweet-smelling pillowcase
When you melt perfectly into the cool sheets
That have been waiting for you all day

INTERLUDE V

He's like submerging your head underwater
Water reaching through every barrier to brush against skin
Washing worries and even shame away
No part of you overlooked or untouched by His liquid love

INTERLUDE VI

He's like the relief you feel
When you finally have a good cry
After too much time spent
Numbed, lifeless, and dry

INTERLUDE VII

He's like the magic
Of the first kiss
Pure and reciprocated acceptance
But way, way better

INTERLUDE VIII

He's like waking up in the morning without an alarm and
Somehow every pillow is perfectly situated
Peace and stillness hovering in the air
And He's the blanket resting over you too

INTERLUDE IX

He's like that thick, still-warm towel
Fresh from the dryer that
Your mom wrapped around you
When you were little and had just finished your bath

INTERLUDE X

He's like breathing for the first time
Cooling relief to a burning chest
His Spirit invading lungs
That hadn't realized they were holding their breath

148

BREATHING UNDERWATER

I've felt for a long time
That the rapids rise too high, rage too fast
Over my head, above my eyes
Can't breathe, can't see
Then the fire of panic rises within me

But in His River of Love
We are meant to be submerged
We are meant to allow Love to overtake us
And even as currents from other rivers
Threaten to overcome us

We were meant to sink into His Love
We were meant to live under this covering
To escape the other currents
By letting His undertow of liquid love
Douse every flame of panic

We were meant to live here
Within the love, not above it
Like the River's Maker,
It takes being lowly
To breathe underwater

And underwater, He wraps us up from behind
Somehow His embrace opens our lungs—
Breathing Him in when
We thought we were drowning—
His name is our breath: "YHWH"

"Whoever gives an honest answer
kisses the lips."

Proverbs 24:26 ESV

part 2: **THE FATHER'S**

DREAMER,

I promise you
I am more than every dream come true

PROGRESS

I will move you
And it might hurt
And it will be different
But I promise it will be good
For I am full of mercy and
I won't ever leave

YADA ENCOURAGEMENT

I know you, and I love you.
This is Yada, to know you as the Bridegroom knows the Bride —
To know by experience...
I am so proud of you.
I knew you when you were broken and lost
> *I've been faithful to love you*
> *No matter the cost*
I'll never stop chasing you
I'll never stop fighting for you
I'll give you my Heart to fight for others too
> *So they can know Yada*
> *And be healed, like you.*
A Light to the Nations
I am Or Goyim
That's what you will be
It's what you will see
A mother to daughters and sons
> *Who long to be free*
> *Who need to know me*

LENS OF FAVOR

Let the light of my face shine on you
And fill your heart to overflow
So it spills into your veins
And pulses through your fingertips
And rushes up into your eyes
Receiving my glory, letting love arise
This is how you see in a new light

REMINDER

Slow down
You still have time

164

THE EXCHANGE

When you feel overwhelmed by this life
By your heart
I am waiting
Just for you
   To climb into my lap
   Look into my eyes
   Know that it's okay to cry
I can handle all of your emotions and holes
And I'll pour something else
Back into your hands
   I'll never leave you broken
   It's my great pleasure
   I'll always restore
   It's what I do
   I pour (love)
I do not stop pouring when you're full
I give you more than you can handle
And that is overwhelming
   But you can leave my lap
   After you've had your cry
   And pour what I restored
   Into other people's lives

WEEP

Tears are not something you're meant to keep

You will never weep alone

SHEPHERDED

Out of the valley,
Out of the valley,
Come out of the valley and
On to the high places with me

THAWING

My compassion can melt your
Frozen-blue-gray and
Bloodless self-protected heart
But if you want me to do surgery,
I must have a raw heart to work with
Wounds like these take time to heal
Little One, will you let me in?
          Will you trust me?

DESIGNER

You were designed
I had you specifically in mind
You were made for this moment

DECISION POINT

This is the River
It's time to jump in

To see what's been broken
It's time to take time to mend

It's time to take time
To start healing within.

VULNERABILITY

Love is allowing yourself to be loved.
It is allowing yourself to be weak,
        And even there,
        Being filled with my peace

EXHAUSTING-FALSE-REST

Know in this moment
There is the space that you need
>*To just breathe*
>*And be with me*
There is space to let go — you can use the word "no"
>*Stop using the filter you use for everyone else*
>*Stop using the tight-fitting "I'm fines"*
>*And always needing everything to fit perfectly right on the line*
>>*Or the rhyme*
>>*Perfection like that doesn't matter to me anyway*

MORNING MOON

Do you ever wonder why the moon stays in the sky
Long after the sun comes up?
Maybe imagine the look in my eyes as the Father
When my Spirit gets to live in you
The moon is jealous, and it takes after its Maker.

ON COMPASSION III

You ask, "Why do I feel so big and so deep?"
Darling,

> *You feel big and you love big*
> *It only makes sense*
> *In this way you resemble the Son*

You were made to comfort the Master

> *When you feel deeply for His created,*
> *To the least you become a great Lover*
> *And this comforts Him.*

TENDERNESS

It makes the magic of your soft, oh, soft eyes shine brighter

CONFESSIONS

May the kisses of my mouth find you in your
most "unredeemable" moments

May shame be far from you when you live inside
these golden rays of my gaze

May fear never keep you from the relief of telling
me what I already know

RELEASED

Little One, you do not have to be perfect for me
You're doing your best
Have you taken time to just be?

WHEN ASKED TO FATHER ME

Little One, when you forget, let me remind you.
When you isolate, let me poke your heart and draw you
Near to me again.
When you need reminding, let me remind you again.
Let me satisfy you in the morning.
Let me wash you in my great delight.

I desire you, and I am close.

INHERITANCE

You're allowed to take time
To listen to your heartbeat
And then listen to mine

COMMUNION QUESTIONS

I am here
Crying with you
Sitting in that
Need-to-cry-can't-cry-because-of-this-or-that
Tension that makes your entire body rigid

I am here
Binding your broken heart
Sitting with you in your
Crying-so-hard-I-can't-even-breathe-or-see,
In the
Is-this-even-okay,
Am-I-even-sane,
Is-this-even-normal
Pain from the world, the people in it

I am here
I will never leave you
You are worth my time
As you sit there and cry

You are worth my affection and you have
My attention

LET GO

Release yourself from having to be "whole" to receive love
It is the letting people love you
That helps you be whole again
Beloved,
Just let it all fall apart

NOT-SO-HYPOTHETICALS

If you are a flower
Let my love water you
If you are a tree
Let my light sustain you
If you are my lover
Let my words be your bread

"The Lord laid the earth's foundations
with wisdom's blueprints.
By his living-understanding all the
universe came into being.
By his divine revelation he broke open
the hidden fountains of the deep,
bringing secret springs to the surface
as the mist of the night dripped down from heaven."

Proverbs 3:19-20 TPT

ALLY LONG

Ally is a lover of the one true Source of connection.
She deeply values this connection in her relationships
as a wife and a friend.

During the nights (and sometimes days) Ally works as
an emergency and trauma certified registered nurse.

In her free time, you can find Ally baking sourdough,
fingerpicking her guitar, or spending time with loved
ones outside. Ally and her husband, Armando, reside
in Huntington Beach, California.

Printed in the USA
CPSIA information can be obtained
at www.ICGtesting.com
CBHW020319060924
13930CB00049B/601

9 781735 081397

honey *learning to live in liquid love*

Tender words have a profound way of making passage
to the deeper depths of the heart.

In Honey, Ally Long chronicles a rich story of
healing, told through poetry, and derived from
communion with God.

Taking things of earth – flowers, trees, homes –
paired with matters of the heart – healing, grief,
compassion – Long has assembled a body of poetry
that reflects the love and hope of the Eternal God.

This call-and-response series of poetry beckons
readers into contemplation; inviting conversation
with God and offering a unique glimpse into beauty,
found in the words of Love.

ISBN 978-1-7350813-9-7

9 781735 081397

90000